WEATHER WATCH

Heatwave
CAUSES AND EFFECTS

Philip Steele

Franklin Watts
London   New York   Sydney   Toronto

© 1991 Zoë Books Ltd

Devised and produced by
Zoë Books Limited
15 Worthy Lane
Winchester
Hampshire SO23 7AB
England

First published in 1991
in Great Britain by
Franklin Watts Ltd
96 Leonard Street
London EC2A 4RH

First published in Australia by
Franklin Watts Australia
14 Mars Road
Lane Cove
New South Wales 2066

ISBN 0 7496 0439 5

A CIP catalogue record for this book is available from the British Library.

Printed in the United Kingdom

Design: Jan Sterling
Picture researcher: Jennifer Johnson
Illustrators: Tony Kenyon, Gecko Ltd

Photograph acknowledgements

Cover: (outer) Graham Harris / Tony Stone Worldwide, (inner) Leslie Howling / Ace Photo Agency.
Pp1 The Telegraph Colour Library, p3 The Telegraph Colour Library, p4 J Allan Cash, p5 Hylden- Liaiso / Frank Spooner Pictures, p7 NASA / Science Photo Library, p10 Barry Waddams, p13 Dennis Firminger / Planet Earth Pictures, p14 Heilman / ZEFA Picture Library, p15 x 3 Barry Waddams, p16 Philippe Plailly / Science Photo Library, p17 Gamma / Frank Spooner Pictures, p18 APL / ZEFA Picture Library, p19 Dave Currey / NHPA, p21 M van Nostrand / Frank Lane Picture Agency, p23 Charlie Nairn / Hutchison Library, p24 Hutchison Library, p25 J Allan Cash Photo Library, p26 Christine Osborne / Mepha / Frank Spooner, p28 Warren Williams / Planet Earth Pictures, p 29 Professor David Hall / Science Photo Library.

Contents

Long, hot days

In hot countries, people dream of rain or snow. When every day is dry and dusty, the thought of cool weather is refreshing. On the other hand, people in cooler countries long for warm summer days and sunshine. They plan holidays in places where they will get as much sunny weather as possible.

Heatwaves bring their own problems from sunburn to lack of water. However, to most people, a long spell of hot weather offers a chance to relax and have fun outdoors.

From time to time in the cooler countries, there is a **heatwave.** This is a long period of hot weather, caused by a large high pressure mass of air either staying in one place or moving very slowly across the land. Since air in such a large mass stays at much the same temperature all the time, few clouds form. This means that the skies stay clear, and the Sun beats down, often for weeks at a time.

A farmer anxiously examines his crop after weeks of drought in the American state of North Dakota.

Day after day is sunny, and at first everyone enjoys the fine weather. Then, gradually, the cities grow hot and sticky, and working becomes uncomfortable. Heatwaves are not welcomed by farmers and gardeners either, since crops and plants need regular rainfall. As the heat continues, plants begin to wilt and the soil turns to dust. Streams dry up and the amount of water stored in reservoirs begins to fall and cause concern.

If the heatwave goes on for a long time, a **drought** may be declared. In some places, this means that people cannot use a sprinkler to water the garden, or a hose to wash the car. Water can be rationed during severe drought.

Weather checks

▼ This map shows the world's main grain-producing areas today. Global warming would change the weather all over the world and affect the types of crops that could be grown in each region in the future. Some regions would become wetter, others would become drier.

Many scientists believe that the air around our planet is becoming hotter, leading to changes in the world's climate. They call this change **global warming**. Scientists are concerned that global warming could change our way of life. It could affect our food, our health and our environment. If rain does not fall when it normally does, crops will fail and people will not have enough to eat. If the temperature rises, it could melt some of the ice at the Poles. This would mean that sea levels would rise and low-lying land would be flooded.

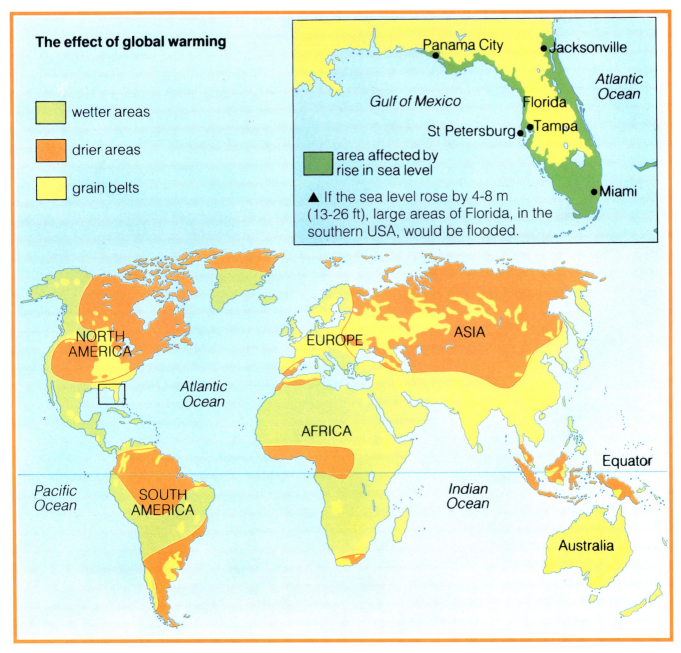

The effect of global warming

wetter areas

drier areas

grain belts

Panama City • • Jacksonville

Gulf of Mexico Florida *Atlantic Ocean*

St Petersburg • • Tampa

area affected by rise in sea level

▲ If the sea level rose by 4-8 m (13-26 ft), large areas of Florida, in the southern USA, would be flooded.

• Miami

NORTH AMERICA

EUROPE ASIA

Atlantic Ocean

AFRICA

Equator

Pacific Ocean SOUTH AMERICA

Indian Ocean

Australia

Heat from space

The Earth is 150 million km (93 million mi) away from the Sun, whose rays of heat and light reach and warm our planet. Although most of the Sun's heat is absorbed by the **atmosphere**, enough filters through to keep plants, animals and humans alive. If the Earth was any nearer to the Sun, its surface would boil and burn. If it was further away, the Earth would freeze.

Sometimes dark areas known as **sunspots** appear on the surface of the Sun. No one yet knows exactly what causes them. Some scientists think that there is a connection between the appearance of sunspots and the type of weather we have on Earth. This is because, about every 11th year, more sunspots appear and there are more violent storms on Earth.

The surface of the Sun is a huge, swirling mass of very hot gases. Great tongues and arches, thousands of kilometres long, flare out into space.

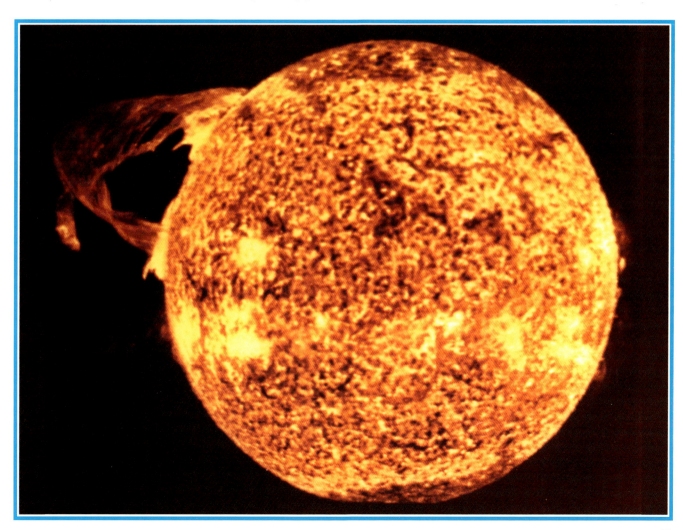

Light and warmth

Some parts of the Earth receive more light and warmth from the Sun than others. Near the Equator, in **equatorial** and **tropical** regions, the Sun shines straight down, and in those parts it is normally very hot during the day. The **polar** regions receive less light and warmth than anywhere else on Earth. The Sun's rays lose more heat as they approach the North and South Poles. They are spread over a wide area and are weaker. This is why the polar regions are always covered in ice and snow.

As the Earth orbits the Sun, different parts of the Earth lean towards the Sun. This tilt gives us our seasons.

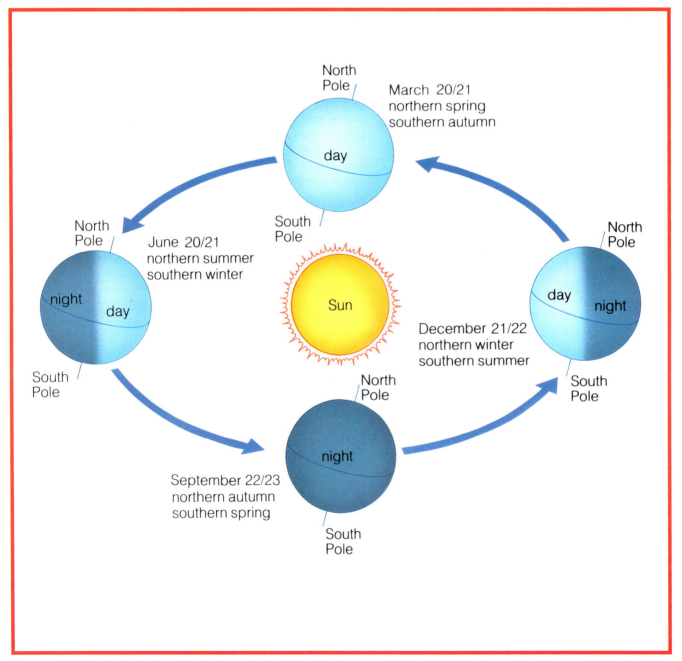

North Pole
March 20/21
northern spring
southern autumn
day
South Pole

North Pole
June 20/21
northern summer
southern winter
night
day
South Pole

Sun

North Pole
day
night
December 21/22
northern winter
southern summer
South Pole

North Pole
night
September 22/23
northern autumn
southern spring
South Pole

The Earth takes a whole year to travel around the Sun. It spins around on its axis once in every 24 hours as well. This gives daytime to the side facing the Sun and night-time to the side away from the Sun. The Earth's axis is tilted. Parts of the planet warm up as they tilt towards the Sun, and cool down as they tilt away. As the tilt changes, so the **season** changes from winter to summer. The northern half of the world has summer in June, July and August. Summer in the southern half is in December, January and February.

Measuring heat

Heat is, in fact, energy - that is, the power to do work or drive machines. One measurement of heat is the calorie, which is the amount of heat needed to raise the temperature of one gram of water by one degree **Celsius**. Another similar measurement is the British thermal unit (Btu), which is the amount of heat needed to raise the temperature of one pound of water by one degree **Fahrenheit**.

Temperatures are measured in degrees by a thermometer: a glass tube with a bulb at the bottom filled either with a silvery liquid metal called mercury, or with alcohol. Both mercury and alcohol **expand** as they get warm. This expansion causes the liquid to rise up the tube.

The scale on a thermometer can be either Celsius or Fahrenheit. On the Celsius scale, water freezes at 0° and boils at 100°. On the Fahrenheit scale, water freezes at 32° and boils at 212°. To turn degrees Celsius into degrees Fahrenheit, multiply them by 1.8 then add 32°. To turn degrees Fahrenheit into degrees Celsius, subtract 32°, then multiply them by 0.556.

How hot does it get?

Every day for a week, make a note of the temperature at, say, 8.15 am, 12.15 pm, 4.15 pm and 8.15 pm. By how much do the temperatures differ during the day? When is it hottest? Does the temperature at, say, 12.15 pm vary throughout the week? By how much?

Hot weather

During a heatwave, the days are calm, with no strong winds. The air usually moves very little. In the middle of the heatwave area, the air presses heavily against the Earth's surface. This is called a centre of high pressure or an **anticyclone**.

The air around the centre of the high-pressure area moves in a spiral. In the northern half of the world, this air turns in a clockwise direction, and in the southern half of the world, it moves anti-clockwise. Sometimes part of the anticyclone expands to cover a long, narrow area, producing a **ridge** of high pressure. Anticyclones bring fine, dry weather, cold in winter but hot in summer.

Low-pressure areas are called **depressions**. These also spiral around, but in the opposite direction to an anticyclone. Depressions bring clouds, rain and high winds, but they can also bring warm weather. This is because the clouds sometimes act as a blanket around the Earth, holding in its warmth and making the air humid and occasionally thundery.

As the Sun sets, a blanket of clouds moves in.
A depression is moving in, bringing rain.

A rain shadow desert

wind carries rain from the ocean

mountain barrier

rain shadow

Clouds form as moist winds rise over a mountain range. Rain is heavy on the seaward side of the mountains. Beyond, the air descends and becomes warmer. This is the rain shadow area where deserts are formed by the drying winds.

Sea and mountains

The oceans and landscape both have an important effect on weather conditions as a whole. When the Sun shines on seas and lakes, surface water **evaporates**, turning into an invisible gas called **water vapour**. Warm air rises so it takes the water vapour with it. As the air rises, it cools and the water vapour turns back into liquid droplets, forming clouds or rain.

A depression moving in from the sea is sometimes blocked by mountains along the coast. The air is forced to rise. It grows cooler very quickly, and the water vapour it contains turns to rain or snow which falls on the mountain slopes that face the sea. By the time the air reaches the other side of the mountains, it has hardly any moisture left in it. The land there is in a **rain shadow**. It gets very little rain and is often very hot and dry.

Mountains also cast real shadows, shielding parts of the valleys from the rays of the Sun. The land lying in the shadows can be very cold indeed.

11

Around the world

The weather in a particular place or country usually has a pattern over the years and this is known as its **climate**. The movements of high and low **air pressure** areas around our planet also follow a regular pattern. The hot air in equatorial regions constantly rises, creating low-pressure areas and giving those regions a hot, damp climate. In the Arctic and Antarctic, around the Poles, the cool air sinks, giving high pressure. There the climate is cold and dry.

The lands with the hottest climate lie around the Equator.

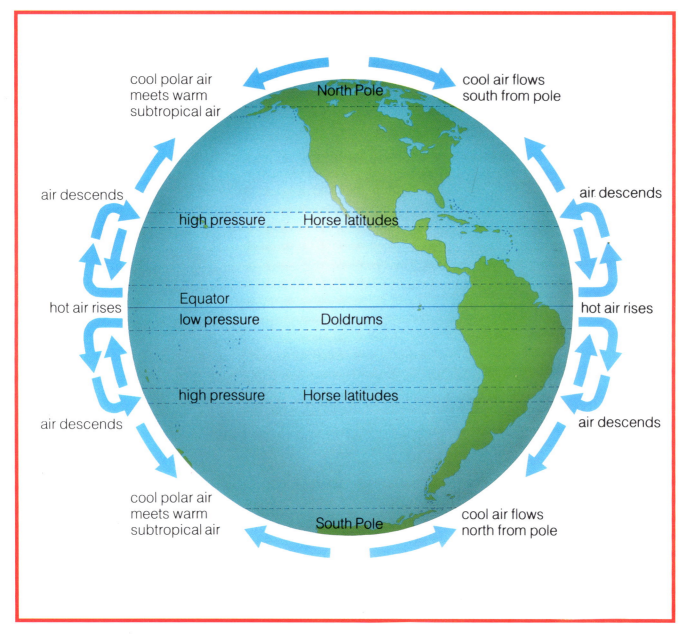

cool polar air meets warm subtropical air

cool air flows south from pole

North Pole

air descends

air descends

high pressure   Horse latitudes

hot air rises

Equator

low pressure   Doldrums

hot air rises

high pressure   Horse latitudes

air descends

air descends

cool polar air meets warm subtropical air

South Pole

cool air flows north from pole

Wet and dry

In most parts of the tropics, ocean winds bring heavy rains for a few months each year. There is a dry season and a wet season. For example, in India there is a monsoon season, when the rainfall is very heavy indeed. In other parts of the tropics there is sometimes no rain at all. A drought may last for many years, turning the land into desert.

The lands around the Sahara Desert, in North Africa, suffer from continual heatwaves. Herds of goats graze the little vegetation that remains, even if it means climbing high into a tree to strip the leaves from the branches. Once all the plants have gone, there is nothing left to trap moisture in the soil and the semi-fertile soil may turn to desert.

✳ In parts of the Sahara Desert in North Africa, the Sun shines for 93 per cent of the total daylight hours, between dawn and dusk.

✳ In 1922 a temperature of 58°C (136°F) in the shade was recorded in the Sahara Desert, in Libya.

Between the polar regions and the tropics lie the **temperate** regions, where the climate is mild. It is rarely very hot or very cold. Both anticyclones and depressions drift across the land, one after the other. Sometimes this pattern changes and a hot weather system lingers for a long time, becoming a heatwave.

Weather signs

A heatwave can be an anxious time for farmers. If water supplies dry up, cattle will go thirsty. Hot weather that lasts too long with no rain can dry up fruit and vegetable crops.

The weather has always been a matter of life and death for sailors. A heatwave means little or no wind. So, sailing ships that used to cross the oceans with their cargoes could be becalmed for days in mid-ocean. During this time both food and water could run out.

Combine harvesters cross the American prairies, one of the world's main wheat-growing regions. Many of the farmer's jobs depend on fine, clear weather conditions. In the old days farmers had to forecast weather conditions for themselves, by checking cloud shapes and wind directions.

Watching the sky

During a heatwave, the only clouds to be seen will probably be very high and wispy. Cirrus clouds, at over 5 km (3 mi) up in the atmosphere, are made of ice crystals. They look like mares' tails in the sky. If they are followed by the hazy, white sheet clouds called cirro-stratus, there will be a change in the weather.

Cirrus clouds (top left) are wispy. Cumulus clouds (bottom left) are puffy. The sky in the picture on the right contains a hazy sheet of cirro-stratus and the blotchy pattern of cirro-cumulus.

Cumulus clouds are lower in the sky and look like puffs of cotton wool. Although small cumulus clouds are quite common during fine weather, if they grow into huge towering columns, thunderstorms are on the way.

Cirro-cumulus clouds are often seen high in the sky during fine weather. These clouds produce a mackerel sky because the small white clouds look like the pattern on a fish's back. "Three days dry, mackerel sky, rain nearby" says one old proverb, and these signs mean that the heatwave is about to break and there will be rain.

Keep a record

About 300 years ago, many people began to keep their own weather records. Today, these give us useful information about the weather in the days before there were official forecasts. Start keeping your own "weather diary", noting the weather conditions every day.

Find out the average temperature and rainfall for your area. Check the last heatwave - when did it start and how long did it last? How did it affect your area? Find out about your local wind directions. Which bring rainy weather and which bring fine weather?

Forecasts and records

Weather instruments

Temperatures day by day are always high in a heatwave. To see how the temperature varies during a particular day, meteorologists use a maximum and minimum thermometer.

Other instruments used are barometers, to measure air pressure, and anemometers, which measure wind speed. Another type of thermometer, a wet and dry bulb thermometer, measures **humidity**, and rain gauges measure the amount of rainfall.

Farmers can now receive regular weather forecasts based on scientific calculations, so they no longer need to remember old sayings. At **weather stations** all round the world, **meteorologists** record details of daily weather conditions. Ships, planes and balloons also collect weather information. Satellites circle the Earth, sending back photographs showing the cloud patterns and the movements of anticyclones and depressions around the planet.

All these details are collected together by the forecasters and used to prepare weather charts. Simplified weather charts are shown on television giving wind directions and expected temperatures. The forecaster explains the chart, pointing out areas of high pressure where there is very little wind and high temperatures which means a heatwave.

Balloons can be used to take weather recording instruments high into the atmosphere. They can also be used to gather information on the effects of pollution, like this balloon released by scientists in the Arctic.

Heat and landscape

As the Sun shines on the Earth's surface, rocks split because of repeated heating and cooling and soil dries out, slowly crumbling into dust and grit. Then strong winds blast the dust and grit against the rocks, breaking them up and wearing them down still further. This process is called **weathering**.

During a heatwave, the water level in rivers, lakes and reservoirs drops. If the hot weather goes on very long they may even dry up.

The floor of a dried-up reservoir during a heatwave.

* In the last 10 years, the Sahara Desert has been advancing southwards by about 100 m (328 ft) a year in places.

* In Namibia, in south-west Africa, reservoirs are filled with sand. The water is stored beneath the sand and is drained off into a well as it is needed. This type of storage prevents too much water being lost through evaporation.

As trucks thunder across the Australian outback, they throw up a long trail of dust. In hot weather, soil is no longer bound together by moisture. It soon forms dust, which is often carried long distances by the wind.

During a long drought, plants die and their roots no longer hold the soil together. It blows away, and the area temporarily becomes a **dustbowl**. This happened in the prairie states of the United States in the 1930s. A series of droughts, combined with attempts to grow too many crops, made the land useless for farming.

If the climate of the world becomes drier and hotter, as many scientists believe it will, whole regions may turn into deserts. In many parts of the world today, existing deserts are growing larger. Even countries, such as Spain, have a serious problem with **desertification**, and a long heatwave can make it worse.

Shrubs, trees and special grasses are now being planted around desert regions to trap moisture and bind the soil. This is being done in places as far apart as China and Nigeria. Water is sometimes taken to desert areas by canal or by pipeline.

Heatwaves and nature

Plants that live in areas that are always hot have developed ways to survive. Some have long roots that reach down to take in water from damper soil far below. Others have hairy stems which trap the morning dew. Desert plants are especially tough. Cacti store moisture in their spiny stems. Other plants, called succulents, have moist, fleshy leaves with a tough skin.

Agave plants are succulents. Their leaves store moisture, and have a waxy surface to prevent water loss. The spines on the leaves prevent thirsty animals from chewing them.

All life on our planet depends on the Sun for its survival. However, too much heat can kill plants and animals. One problem is that water supplies may dry up. Plants in temperate lands are less well-suited to heat. Water makes up over 90 per cent of some plants and without it, plants cannot stay upright. They droop and the leaves curl up, desperately trying to hold in moisture.

A long heatwave can cause a lot of damage. Twigs, leaves or grass can become so dry that just a spark can start a fire. Fires kill wild animals and birds as well as trees.

Heat and water

Plants need heat, light and water to live. First of all, find out how different amounts of heat affect growing plants by preparing two trays full of seeds, such as mustard and cress. Put one in a cold place and one in a warm place and see which seeds sprout first.

To find out how much water is needed, try giving a potted plant varied amounts over several weeks. Give it a lot one day, leave it until the soil has been dry for some days, then give it half the amount, then quarter the amount.

How does the plant react? Does it droop or lose leaves? Do its leaves change colour? Find out which country the plant you have chosen comes from. Is it suited to a wet or a dry climate?

The fennec is a little fox that lives in North Africa. Its big ears are part of a body-cooling system which helps it to survive extreme temperature. Its feet have hairy soles which help to spread its weight when walking on soft sand. The fennec fox avoids the heat of the day and hunts by night.

Animals in the heat

In order to survive, animals must **adapt** to the climates in which they live. For example, frogs and fish sometimes bury themselves in river mud during the dry season and wait for the rains to come. Mammals in temperate lands moult, shedding fur or hair in order to stay cool in the summer months.

During a drought, wild animals often die as they search in vain for water. Farm animals need special attention when there is a heatwave. Lack of water can lead to cattle dying if a well or river dries up.

Pets are particularly at risk during a heatwave. Make sure that they are given enough water to drink, and that they are protected from too much heat. Never leave a dog in a car without first opening the window. Wild birds need water as well. During a heatwave put out a bowl of water for the birds that visit your garden.

The need for water

Many animals thrive only in very moist conditions.

Fill a seed tray with soil and leaves. Water one half of it and place a cover over that half. Leave the other half dry and put the tray outside on a hot day. Find some snails and put them in the tray. Notice which half they choose. (Don't forget to return the snails to where you found them.)

Look around a park or garden during a heatwave. Creatures such as snails and slugs are still there, but they are hiding. See if you can find them.

Heat and humans

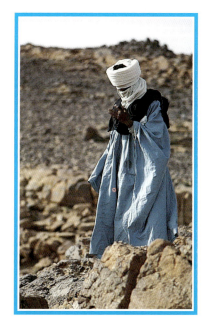

People who live in the desert have learned how to survive in the heat. Men of the Tuareg people, who live in the Sahara, wear robes which allow cool air to flow around the body. They wind veils around their heads to protect them from the Sun and to keep out the sand and dust.

Like other living creatures, humans depend on the Sun for warmth and food. However, too much heat or sunlight is bad for us as well. People sometimes faint in very hot weather and can die if their internal body temperature rises above 41°C (106°F). In the United States alone, about 150 people die from heatstroke each year. A lack of water is even more disastrous, since humans can live only a short time without water.

Humans are warm-blooded and we are able to control our body temperature. Warm blood is carried around the body by small tubes called blood vessels. In order to lose heat, the blood vessels near the surface of the body widen. This makes more blood flow close to the surface and heat passes from the warm blood through the skin through small holes, or pores, making fair-skinned people look red in the face. Water also comes to the surface as sweat, and this cools the body as well.

Skin protection

People whose families originally came from very hot countries have black or brown skin, which gives them protection against the rays of the Sun. People from temperate lands have pale skin that burns easily. During a heatwave, pale-skinned people should either cover up bare skin, or rub in a special cream that blocks out the harmful rays. Too much sunbathing can make the skin dry and wrinkled, and sometimes cause skin cancer.

Heat and food

Heatwaves cause humans other problems. Food goes bad more quickly in hot weather. This is because tiny organisms called bacteria spread more easily in warm food. Until refrigerators were invented in the nineteenth century, food had to be stored in cool rooms or boxes of ice. Today, many people can store or freeze food through the hottest weather.

✻ In the 1930s, there were so many heatwaves in parts of the United States that 15,000 people died of heatstroke.

✻ The human body is made of about 66 per cent water.

✻ Sunlight is not always harmful. It helps the body to make vitamin D, keeping the bones and teeth healthy.

The loss of crops and livestock can put human life at risk. One long drought in Australia lasted from 1964 to 1966. Nearly 33 per cent of the wheat crop was lost, and 20 per cent of the country's sheep died.

In less developed countries which already have dry climates, droughts may be very severe and bring famine. Thousands of people may die of thirst and hunger. Old people and babies are particularly at risk. In recent years disasters have occurred in many regions of Africa and Asia. Emergency supplies of food and water can help save lives, but new methods of farming and saving water are the only long-term solution.

A supply of water is brought to villagers during a severe drought in Ethiopia. During hot weather, people need to drink more water than usual. Lack of water, or dehydration, can cause death.

Living with heat

Houses have to protect the people who live in them against heat just as much as against cold. Houses along the Mediterranean coast are often painted white, as this reflects the Sun's heat from the buildings. In tropical regions, a shaded platform or verandah is sometimes built around the outside of the house so that people can catch whatever breeze there is.

The white walls of this house in Spain help to keep it cool inside.

Many buildings in the Republic of Yemen are made of dried mud. The windows are small. These buildings are designed to keep cool in the desert heat.

In desert areas, houses must be built near a water supply. At an oasis, trees can be planted for shade. Dried mud or adobe can be used to make bricks. Building with adobe bricks helps to keep houses cool. The windows are small and few, just enough to let in light, but not too much heat.

Modern buildings in very hot areas may have windows with tinted glass, and be fitted with air conditioning to filter out the dust and keep the air cool. Electric fans are used to create a fresh breeze.

Materials and structures

Unusually high temperatures affect building materials. Architects and engineers have to consider this when designing and building anything from houses to bridges. Many bridges are made of steel, which expands slightly in hot weather. To make the bridge safe, expansion joints are fitted. The joints allow sections of the bridge to move very slightly as the steel expands.

Roads can also be affected during a heatwave. In hot, dry weather, the surface of the road often bakes hard and cracks open. Asphalt roads can be permanently damaged when the Sun melts the tar.

Today, building materials have to be tested to see how they will be affected by heat. Materials that catch fire easily in dry conditions have to be avoided.

Cool, cooler, coolest

Which materials carry, or conduct, heat the best?

Find examples of the following materials: wood, metal, stone, glass, plastic and brick. Lay them out in the hot sunshine. After two hours, which ones feel cool to the touch? Which ones feel hot?

If you were building a house, which material would you use, and why?

Making use of sunshine

These pools of sea water are in the Canary Islands. The heat of the Sun evaporates the water, leaving behind the salt that it contains. It is then raked up into piles and packed for use.

People have always tried to find different ways in which sunshine can be used. The Sun's drying power has been used for a long time. Before freezers were invented, most fish, meat and fruit was preserved by drying. Grapes that are dried in the Sun become raisins. In some countries today, tanks are filled with sea water and as this evaporates in the sunshine, piles of salt are left behind.

Solar cells can turn sunlight into electrical power. This could become a valuable source of energy in sunny regions of the world. This solar cooker can bake a cake in 50 minutes.

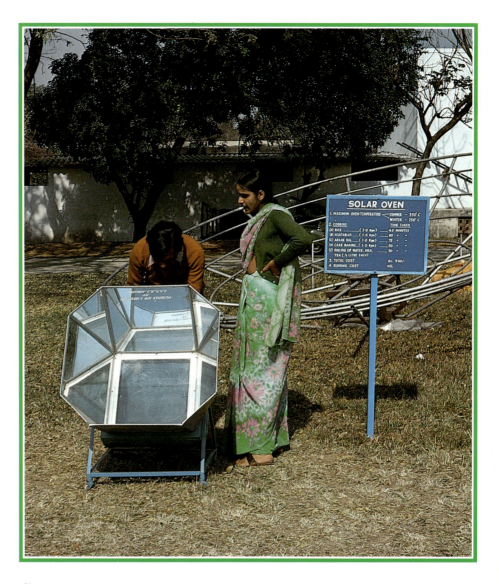

Sun power

The Earth receives a huge amount of energy from the Sun but nearly all of it goes to waste. However, more and more use is being made of **solar power.** The heat from the Sun falls on metal panels attached to the roof or walls of a house. Water piped through the panels heats up and can be used to give hot water or warm the house.

Alternatively, a material called silicon can be used to make **solar cells** that turn sunlight into electric current. The electricity can be used to power calculators and street lights.

Solar power is not a cheap form of power but it has its advantages. It does not poison the atmosphere, nor is it dangerous.

Glossary

adapt   To alter or change to suit a different purpose or different surroundings.

air pressure   The force with which air presses down on the surface of the Earth.

anticyclone   An area of high air pressure.

atmosphere   The layer of gases which make up the air around the planet.

axis   An imaginary line joining the North Pole and the South Pole through the centre of the Earth.

Celsius   The official name for a Centigrade temperature scale, invented by the Swedish astronomer Anders Celsius (1701-1744).

climate   The average weather conditions of an area over a period of time.

depression   An area of low air pressure.

desertification   The turning of dry grasslands into desert.

drought   A long period with little or no rainfall.

dustbowl   An area where the upper layers of the soil blow away.

equatorial   Belonging to the area around the Equator, the imaginary line drawn around the middle of the globe.

evaporate   To turn into vapour.

expand   To swell or grow larger.

Fahrenheit   A scale of temperature invented by the German scientist Gabriel Daniel Fahrenheit (1686-1736), who first used mercury in thermometers.

global warming   A change in climate in which the air around the planet is warmed by the burning of fuels and the use of certain chemicals.

heatwave   A long period of unusually hot dry weather.

humidity   The amount of moisture found in the air.

meteorologist   Someone who makes a scientific study of weather conditions.

polar   To do with the areas around the North and South Poles, the Arctic and Antarctic.

rain shadow   A dry area shielded from rainy winds by a mountain range.

ridge   A long, narrow band of high pressure air .

season   One of the periods into which the year is divided, according to the weather conditions.

solar cell   A device which uses sunlight to make electricity.

solar power   The use of the Sun's energy to provide heating, or to generate electricity.

sunspot   An area of the Sun's surface where the gases are at a lower temperature.

temperate   Describes a mild climate in which the weather is never very hot, nor very cold.

tropical   Situated within the band on either side of the Equator where the Sun passes directly overhead.

water vapour   An invisible gas created when water evaporates.

weathering   The wearing down of the landscape by wind, rain, frost, ice and heat.

weather station   A base where all kinds of weather conditions are scientifically recorded.

Index